PREVENT

THE

RESENT

A GUIDE FOR THE ENGAGED OR NEWLY MARRIED COUPLE

Venice J. Davidian

ISBN 978-1625121059

Copyright @ 2012 by Venice J. Davidian

Published by Tutor Turtle Press LLC, 1027 S. Pendleton St., Suite B-10, Easley, SC 29642.

www.TutorTurtlePress.com

Cover design by:

Lynda Colón
FREELANCE GRAPHIC DESIGN &
MARKETING COMMUNICATIONS
www.fgdmc.com

. . . This is simply a tool; a tool that has been formed from years of discussion, problems, arguments, discoveries, disastrous and wondrous moments . . .

. . . You'll enjoy a marriage that is flowing and not stagnant. You'll enjoy a relationship that does not chip away at your personas or your dreams, fantasies, and ambitions;... you will have a relationship that blossoms, one that flows and ebbs . . .

. . . A relationship that encourages the good and the beautiful to grow from it, and from each of you . . .

I DO!

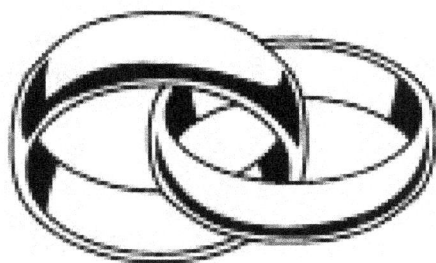

Well,
I don't!

TABLE OF CONTENTS

I do!

Sorry I don't.

I thought you did.

You're wrong, I don't!!

Sound familiar? Maybe not at this point in your marital career, but sooner or later, in the early stages of your marriage, as new situations, circumstances, or occurrences arise, these will be the very words that you'll exchange. The classic difference of opinion.

Some of these differences are inevitable. You are two different people and your ideas, thoughts, and opinions are going to differ. Is it going to be an all out brawl? Does it have to be a knockdown, drag out "fight"? The answer is no. What's going to end up getting you, creating a wedge between the two of you, and possibly destroying the beautiful relationship you once had, are the little things. Yes, the little things. The very things that we discuss in this book.

PREVENT THE RESENT

Most of these "little things" that I'm referring to begin as expectations. The "little things" become a problem when these expectations do not get met. Unmet expectations can then cause resentments.

Very simply put, **an unmet expectation equals a resentment**. Sounds simple, I know, but this entire premise can be very elusive. It can creep in without us even knowing that it exists. Again, these "little things" are the byproducts that come about because aspects of the relationship have not been discussed, have not been brought to light prior or during the marriage; therefore, have remained unspoken, unmet expectations.

Expectation is being defined here as "a picture that I have of how I think something *should* be." The expectation must be addressed, it must be verbalized to then turn it from this picture you have way back somewhere in your brain, into a tangible part of your marriage. Instead of playing a guessing game, you both should know what each other *expects* in <u>as many</u> situations as possible.

You need to prevent the resentment from ever taking shape. There is no way a couple can know, until being married for a while, that issues like the ones that we present even exist, or that they could possibly cause a problem later on.

What we are attempting to do here in this book is to try to prevent this resentment from ever entering into the blissful marital setting.

To do this, we present to you many different topics to discuss in depth in order to address your expectations; therefore, dispel your resentments. The topics that we'll be discussing are the hurdles that must be approached and mastered, or they will cause marital riffs.

You might be saying that, in fact, you want some unvoiced expectations so that your partner can fulfill them and thus lead you to be pleased. Nice sentiment. You'll be lucky if that happens a couple of times. **Reality check**. That's a game. You play, you lose. How do I know? What are this lady's credentials, you ask? One failed marriage and one strong marriage, and stumbling head on with everything in between. At some point, I stopped and realized what most of the "little things" were and put them down on paper. What's presented in this book is the outcome of years and years of being faced with hurdles, disagreements, fights, misunderstandings, and hurt feelings. Also, years and years of trying to get through all of that by communication, and trial and error. Only to realize after all is said and done, that most of the ugliness could have been avoided if only there had been some type of outline or blueprint that my partner and I could have used to more closely familiarize ourselves with some universal subjects that emerge in marriages and take you quite by surprise. Subjects that, because you are taken by surprise, (you've never talked about it before with your partner) put you on the defensive and ultimately cause the resentment and therefore the "fights".

This is a How To book, if you will. Not a *How to Have a Perfect Marriage* book, but a *How to Start Off in a*

Marriage Knowing More About Myself and My Spouse So We'll Have More of a Capacity to Cope With the Obstacles That Surely Will Arise book.

I do try to cover many subjects so maybe some of these topics will seem generally familiar to you or you may think, gee, we already talked about this. Even when that seems to be the case, it still won't hurt to at least acquaint yourselves with how the subject matter is being presented. You may learn something new. Remember in the first paragraph, I chose to call your relationship a "marital career"? That's because a marriage is work. It's also fun, companionship, pleasure, excitement, and about as many other nouns as you can possibly think of. But, it is work. It takes a lot of effort to make a marriage flourish and grow.

The very same kind of effort that hopefully you will be putting into how the two of you get through this manual.

Heard it all before, right? "It's the little things that matter in a marriage." Well, it's true. One little argument about one little subject stacked on top of the other. One little resentment caused from one little unmet expectation placed on top of the other, just like a child's hand-over-hand game, your marriage is on the bottom and each resentment gets piled on it until, poof, it all crumbles. And so do the two of you!

"Irreconcilable differences, Your Honor." That's what it's called in the divorce court. Irreconcilable differences. Translated, this really means that stuff is happening between the two of you that you can't seem to agree on; therefore, are arguing about. Stuff that you're probably arguing a lot about. It could be big stuff, little stuff, but it's stuff. Stuff that creeps in and causes differences, which in turn causes wedges between the two of you and ultimately causes a breakdown of the marriage.

"Oh, that won't happen to us, we're too much in love," you say. I'm sure you are very much in love or you wouldn't be embarking on this marriage quest to begin with, what with all the statistics so incredibly against you. According to a leading cultural index, the divorce rate in 2009 was 3.4% per 1000 in the US (*Statistical Abstract of the United States*, 2012, US Census Bureau. US Dept. of Commerce, Economics & Statistics Admin. Table 133). I'm sure you've also heard numbers like one out of three marriages end in divorce or that one out of five end up in counseling. Do you want your marriage to end up as a statistic? A lot of times marriages end over big stuff, stuff that's down right terrible like spousal abuse. But a lot of times marriages end because these two, at one point, very much in love people, haven't taken the time to introspect on important issues and haven't dedicated themselves to preparing their life's path to include their partner's viewpoint.

A marriage, defined by me, is the union of two people, legally, spiritually, and physically. But really, what does that mean? What exactly does marriage mean to you? Have you taken the time to think about this? To ingest this? We use the term quite freely; Hey, I'm getting married! Hey, when are you getting married? Are you married? What does it mean? Do I or we look at marriage as a noun, a thing? Do we look at it as a verb, an action?

What does marriage mean to me, to us? You **must** stop and ask this. This is so incredibly basic but so very important! What are your expectations from your marriage? You need to define them, say them, write them down, and converse with your partner about them. Don't walk into your marriage blindly.

Don't walk into the marriage without having a meaning attached to it; without knowing what you want it to be for you in your life and what you expect from it. You know why? Because otherwise these expectations, these pictures of what you thought your marriage would be like, are left in the mind and soul somewhere and as "stuff" occurs during the marriage that doesn't jive with those repressed, unspoken expectations, you'll feel cheated and empty. Your expectations will be unfulfilled. If, however, you haven't brought those expectations to life, if you haven't made them tangible, then **you** are equally as guilty if they do not get fulfilled in the marriage.

Here is an example. This is one example out a million that I could have chosen. Let's just say that somewhere in the recesses of my mind I have a picture, a fantasy, an **expectation** of my husband, that in our marriage, he will be the pillar of strength. I expect my marriage to be traditional and really expect that my new husband will fill the traditional "strong husband" role. If I don't, number one, bring this into *my* conscious mind and realize that this is, in fact, an expectation of mine, and number two, voice this to my partner to see if this is part of his marital vision, then how will I know that this will either be or not be part of my future?

My new husband could be on a totally different wavelength. He might feel, hey, I'm not going to be the backbone. I don't want any part of traditional roles. I want a two-way street. But he, too, has got to realize this and verbalize it. Or he too will be faced with an unmet expectation from his new wife. Those unmet expectations will cause strife and ill feelings. You're probably saying, yeah, but we already know that about each other. We've been dating and I know what he's like and what kind of husband he'll be, and he knows what kind of wife I'll be. That may be so, but, unless you stop, introspect, declare your wants and discuss them, you may be very surprised and disappointed at some future time. The tricky part is identifying the expectations *before* they become resentments. That's what we try and do here. We'll help you to try to **PREVENT THE RESENT** by helping you identify the topics, show you how to approach them, and the rest is up to you. Some people have tons of expectations. They always have a romantic picture in their heads of how something should be. Some people don't have many.

But, to actually stop and say to a partner, "let's talk about this, this, this, and this, and identify our expectations regarding those topics" is a very difficult thing to do. Not impossible, however.

Identifying "marriage" as **the** main topic to discuss is one of the most important premarital exercises you and your partner will do. Although it may seem so unbelievably simple, unless someone tells you to define marriage, for yourself and for each other as I have, or unless you are a very introspective individual, you probably will not take the time for this. You both need to stop and think and ask yourselves and each other. What does being married really mean to me. What do I want it to mean? What do I want to give to it and what do I want to get out of it?

Much of "being married" is intangible. It's a state of mind, it's a feeling, it's a sensation, and it's a way of living. But, on the other hand, much to do with marriage is very tangible and can really be weighed and measured beforehand as you'll see in our discussions. Think of it this way: Before you accept a job offer, both you and your prospective employer sit and discuss a plethora of information regarding the job. You'd be a fool to walk into a new job blindly. You know you need to be well aware of the job description, the salary, the benefits package, etc. You want to know your product or service and the company. Getting married, or rather the marriage itself should be viewed in somewhat the same way. It should be discussed and pondered from all angles. Obviously there are differences with a marriage and a job.

When a job doesn't work out, you quit, you move on. One can argue, well, if the marriage doesn't work out, you divorce, you move on. Yes, but here's the major difference, of course, you're in love. And that's all the more reason to walk into this with your eyes wide open. There's more at stake. There are feelings, lots of feelings at stake. The chances of those feelings not getting hurt are much better if you do a little work beforehand.

The second thing you and your partner need to do after asking yourselves what you want this marriage to really be for you, is where do you see yourself in respect to the marriage in five or ten years. Again, you've heard that question asked of you at interviews. It's a very valid question. It is also a very difficult one. It requires introspection and self-awareness. I can't tell you how many friends of mine have said that they never would have thought, back when they got married, that things would be the way they are now. Some have said positive things. They've said that they're happy with their marriage. Most everything has turned out as they expected (expectation fulfilled = contentment). Most, however, have been negative. They have said that most aspects of their marriages just plain stink. Nothing has turned out to be what they had expected (unfulfilled expectations = resentment).

This is what we're concerned about in this book. The two of you need to project and set goals for the marriage. You need to tell each other where you see yourselves, in your minds' eye, now and in five or ten years. In your minds' eye this can take on very different forms. It can mean I want to see a family and home. It could mean I want us to be happy, nothing else matters. It could mean lots of money, no kids, and a fast-lane life. You may see a strong emphasis on careers or yearly vacations. Whatever the case may be, the point is, your mind's eye has got to see it and then the two of you must relay it to each other. What if you're seeing two completely different scenarios? Then what? Better to know that now!

It is not an impossibility. It is, however, difficult because it requires time and thought. Can we see everything in our marital future? Of course not. But just like monetary goals, when we diligently save up to acquire that special something, we can set marital goals so that the two of you can work towards that special marriage-something. Doesn't this goal, acquiring a solid marital future, sound like even a more important goal to work towards than some others?

You, as engaged or newly married people absolutely, positively have got to talk about the items that we are about to present.

Some of these things you will have already talked about. Some you will not have even thought about yet. You're getting the heads-up!! I wish that I had been even *slightly* aware of these aspects before my marriage(s). I know what you're saying now..."We've talked about a lot of stuff. We know where we want to live, we know we want children. We both like to golf." Well, it's great that you've begun to discuss these things. But even two relatively benign issues like where you want to live and having or not having kids are so much more involved and intricate.

Scenarios will come into play later on in the marriage that you cannot even imagine at this point in your relationship. That's the reason for this little guide. This will help present to you and your partner many of the problems and issues that could come up along the way of your marriage. If both of you, because of this guide, become even slightly more aware of, number one, your own outlook, your own honest to goodness outlook on a particular matter, and then, number two, your partner's outlook on that particular issue, think of the heartache you might have just saved yourself, your partner, and your marriage. It will have been worth reading. None of us has a crystal ball. We cannot see solidly into the future and we probably wouldn't want to for most, but in this world of uncertainties, tragedies, and failures, when we do finally find something beautiful, when we find love, we want to get it, give it, and want to share it. When this newfound love of ours is special enough to then want to build a life from it, we rejoice and begin to think of marriage.

To actually want to spend your entire life with the same person is, when you really think about it, overwhelming! Why not enter into this beautiful relationship with a little more knowledge, understanding and enlightenment? It has been said that knowledge is power. That is true even when it has to do with intangibles like love and marriage. You'll be equipped, or better equipped with new knowledge about your future partner and more importantly about yourself.

Hopefully, while you are embarking on this marital awareness exercise, you will begin to see that there is a way to approach delicate issues. A discussion, even if it involves differences of opinions, has its own art form. You can be the type that argues right away, or the more passive type who will brush off anything so as not to have a confrontation, or you can fall anywhere in between. Whatever the case is, by going through these exercises, you will have the added bonus of learning how to discuss marital type matters without taxing the relationship or yourself. In the future, remember how you "discussed" those topics in this great little book and do the same then.

Statistics are everywhere about how many marriages end in divorce and how many more end up in expensive counseling. Do you know what happens during those counseling sessions? The once happily married couple ends up talking about things that should have been discussed *before* they got married, or at least early on in the marriage. They talk about topics that they are strongly disagreeing upon, topics that they are arguing over, fighting over, and quite possibly divorcing over. Most of which are the very topics that we urge you to discuss here and now! Is reading this going to give you a foolproof marriage? Are you not going to end up a statistic because you've read this book and discussed everything in it with your significant other? We'd like to think so, but that's not possible. Here is my little disclaimer. Like anything else, this approach is not a guarantee of a magnificent marriage. That's not the intention. That could never be the outcome of this or any marital preparatory text. This is simply a tool; a tool that has been formed from years of discussions, problems, arguments, discoveries, disastrous and wondrous moments. A tool that we offer to you graciously in hopes of helping you both create, have, and maintain, if not always, but for the most part, a wonderful relationship.

You'll enjoy a marriage that is flowing and not stagnant. You'll enjoy a relationship that does not chip away at your personas or your dreams, fantasies, and ambitions; a relationship that doesn't drain you mentally and physically because it requires constant negative energy. Hopefully, you'll have a relationship that blossoms, one that flows and ebbs. One that encourages the good and the beautiful to grow from it, and from each of you.

HOW TO USE THIS MARRIAGE TOOL

Remember first to introspect and answer the important question about what marriage means to you that we began with in the preceding pages. Then when you're ready to move on, read each topic and its introductory text. Get a feel for the topic, begin your own discussion about the subject and then use our discussion points. If you begin your own discussion and it seems to be quite interesting on it's own, go with it. Save our discussion points until you're done with your own. Don't try to go through these points all at once. You need to take time to ingest and digest. Some topics are more delicate and require much more analyzing on your parts. Stay with them, return to them. But remember, if it's in this book, you can rest assured it will make a difference in your marriage. Don't skip any topic. You'll wish you hadn't!!!

You may discover things that you didn't know about your partner, even things that you don't like, don't be accusatory when discussing these things. Many couples get to the point of effectively communicating their thoughts, but then communications break down by bringing in blame statements: "you said", "you always", and "you never". Try to refrain from these statements. These statements hurt and create even more negativity than is already present in an argumentative environment.

Arguing while discussing these issues, although some are very delicate, defeats the purpose of the whole exercise. If a subject seems to be too heavy, leave it alone and come back to it. Think about it for a while. After you've mulled it over, come back and talk about it. Please don't let these discussion topics create problems that weren't there to begin with. But, should you recognize that there are a whole lot of points that you differ on during these discussions, then maybe a light should go off for both of you. Maybe you need to really get some type of professional counseling. Above all, let your love for each other, the foundation that all this is built upon, the reason for this whole party, guide you through this book and through life. This entire text revolves around resentments and the way that resentments can build during the course of a marriage. Earlier I stated that my definition of marital resentments equals unmet emotional and tangible needs, wants, and expectations. Resentments can build even without arguments. One partner might not even realize that the other partner feels resentment towards him/her. Remember that hand over hand game? That's what marital resentments are like. One on top of another and then, without even noticing, the breakdown of the marriage begins.

Resentments are created by unresolved expectations, the unmet need. Think of it. We expect certain things from our partners. Not just material things. We expect them to do certain things, act certain ways, go certain places, say certain things, think in a certain way. Unless we pre-address as many of these matters as possible (like we do in this text) then the partner is completely unaware of your expectations. Therefore, your partner does not carry out as you think he/she should have. BOOM! Instant resentment, instant argument or the makings thereof. Yes, you might put these resentments on the back burner, but there they'll simmer and blow up at another time. When these resentments build up, your partner will feel like you're arguing about something that he/she thought you were in congruency with, but both of you find out you're not! You start to think that, hey, this is not how I wanted this to turn out, or this is not how I wanted to feel in this marriage. You begin to feel unloved and misunderstood. You begin to feel alone and not unified. Your own private definition of marriage begins to break down.

Webster's dictionary defines resentment as " feeling angry or indignant about something or someone." Within the context of marriage, and with regard to this book, I define marital resentment as, (since we live in a predominantly "me" oriented society), "the feeling of anger that results from our partner not meeting up to what we would have expected in a given situation."

In a perfect marriage, or any relationship for that matter, if we were to completely let go of our egos and live day to day putting the other person first in all situations and at all costs, it would never bother us in the least if or when they did or didn't do something that didn't fit our expectations. As a matter of fact, we wouldn't even have the expectations to begin with. But, that idealistic scenario is almost impossible. You and your partner will have expectations. And, because you both will act according to your own agendas, you will both come shy, at times, of meeting those expectations or having them met. When we are at the receiving end of a non-met expectation, we either comply with the situation and harbor our anger and hurt feelings, or we argue and just plain get really angry and begin a slow trip towards resenting our partner.

Think it can't or won't happen to you? Think again. Expectation exists, expectation unfulfilled, resentment. See the pattern?

If neither of the two of you had any preconceived notions or expectations of what you would like your partner's response to a certain matter to be, or if you didn't wishfully view him/her as automatically wanting or needing or feeling the same way as you about matters in life, there wouldn't be any expectations, but you know what? There are always expectations. It's human nature. We just expect that all will see matters in life as we do. Especially when it comes to our spouses. Unfortunately, that is not always going to be the case. Along with the foiled expectations come the resentments that follow. We begin to seriously resent our partners for not seeing things the way we do and these resentments build and build until finally what was once a love begins to turn to a hate and our differences are no longer reconcilable. We begin to feel alone. We begin to feel as if the marriage is one-sided. Will talking about all these matters before the marriage prevent this? One can't guarantee this. But whenever we walk into any situation, especially one as delicate as a marriage, with eyes that have been opened to certain matters, we can view the situation, in this case, the marriage, with a more mature attitude; an attitude that allows for compromising.

If you learn anything from this text, please learn **how** to discuss these issues and others that may come along so that they do not remain *unspoken expectations* and will therefore not become *resentments*. Many of the big resentment causers are included in this book. But even when some other subject arises that smells like it could be a future resentment causer, sniff it out, and meet it head-on with a healthy discussion. Strife in a marriage is inevitable; knowing what to do to prevent it from turning into ugly resentments is not.

All right, ready to begin? Read the topic introduction first. It will include statements and questions. Think about what it's saying to you as an individual first. This is key to a constructive discussion regarding the issue. As new couples, we tend to want to think as one, as a unit. This is a cause of many problems, because inevitably, as time goes by, our own feelings towards a matter must push forward and no longer will we always put the good of the couple before our own needs and desires. You need to do this right from the beginning. What do I want? How do I feel about this issue? This may sound like a selfish attitude and it may sound like it doesn't belong in the marriage scenario, but that couldn't be further from the truth.

You need to be honest with yourself first, right from the very beginning. Should you never bend from your own views, should you never compromise? Hardly. You have to bend or there is no marriage. But start with your own views and then your partner's views. Listen, respect, and then go on to addressing them collectively as a couple. Use the discussion points to enhance your conversation about the particular topic. If other questions, comments, or observations about the topic come into the conversation, that's great, go with it. But try to stick to the topic at hand without getting off that particular track.

You really could begin your married life without all of this analyzing. Entering into your marriage semi-blindly and ignorant to deeper insights, feelings, and desires is completely your prerogative. But if you have a passion for life, if you wish to not just attempt something but really, really live it, and feel it, and be it, then by all means jump into this sea of self and partner exploration and feel the difference it will make in your relationship. Take your time and enjoy getting to know yourself and each other even better than you did.

Good luck and have fun.

FAMILY

FAMILY

This is a very important subject. Let's start here because first and foremost the two of you **are** your new family. I can't emphasize this enough. Keep this concept alive. Emblazon this on your souls. There can be much strife involved in "extended family situations" as you may have already experienced, but there can also be harmony. You and partner and your strength as a new family are the key.

First, let's get the terminology straight. When I say "your family," I speak of your new family, the family that is the fresh unit of you and your spouse/spouse-to-be. I'm very strong on this point and with good reason. For the sake of the strength of your new marriage, <u>refer to yourselves as a family</u>. As strange as that may seem, it will be one of the most important things you will do. Eventually, within you, stemming directly from calling yourselves a family, will grow a sensation of strength and togetherness. Right now, you may not think of each other as a family, and in not doing so, you keep all the wonderful things about being a new family out of the picture. Simply by referring to the marriage and the two of you as a family, you invite in more strength, togetherness, responsibility, and commitment.

The family you came from individually I will refer to as your "family of origin."

I suggest strongly that when you are discussing families, both in respect to this book or in general conversation, that you use this terminology. Using the terminology like this actually helps keep focus on the fact that your family (the two of you) should be separate and central in your minds and conversations. I think you would agree that the healthiest relationships between a married couple stem from a strong sense of unity between partners.

Having said that, let me move on to say why this topic is very important. Early on, a problem can occur when we conjure up in our mind's eye how we would like our partner to react to our family of origin and how we want his family of origin to react to us. This should NOT be the emphasis. Your relationships with your families of origin, and expending energy to satisfy their wants and desires, needs to be secondary to the new family you have created. For example, let's say you're recently married, and a career opportunity arises which involves a relocation across the country. (We'll get into more relocation detail as we move on.) Assuming that both of you see the positives and are willing to relocate to forge your future together, how much influence will you let either family of origin hold in regard to your decision to make the move? Will the family of origin influence that decision because they don't want their child living far away?

Will either of you give substantial credence to that influence? Will you regret doing so later on? The questions and situations may differ, but the themes are generally the same. Whether it's naming your new baby, buying a home, choosing a religion, etc.; many times the power of the family of origin is extremely strong. If either of you have the inclination to let your family of origin exercise influence on these important decisions, or either of you have a desire to satisfy your family of origin's wishes, get this out in the open with your partner NOW.

By placing a central emphasis on your family (the two of you), how the two of you feel about each other's family of origin or how each other's family of origin feels about you is no longer critical. It's still important, but it's no longer the emphasis. Yes, it is a good thing if everyone likes each other, gets along and becomes allies. However, this may or may not happen. What usually happens is that we start off with those very humble feelings where we wonder and so sincerely hope that our partner's family likes us. "Do you think they'll like me?" or "Oh, I hope they like me!" These are very sweet sentiments but unfortunately they are very unrealistic and very immature. We have all felt them and have all ridden the wave of nausea on that first encounter.

These humble, benevolent feelings towards the family of origin of our partner don't last. I'm not implying that no matter what, we will begin to hate our partner's family or they us. But, what I am saying is that those original feelings of desire on your part, for your partner's family to "like you" will disappear. It won't be as grave an issue because you've placed the real emphasis on your new family. That's where the importance lies. This is the groundwork to a very healthy, mature relationship. We will each harbor secret feelings, negative or positive, regarding our partner's family of origin. If they're negative, we tend to let those feelings slide in the beginning of our married life to keep peace and harmony. This results in many misunderstandings, fights, and ill feelings in later years. Many of which could have been avoided. What needs to be done, way in the beginning of your relationship, is, instead of placing all the emphasis on whether or not you'll be liked, the emphasis should be placed on the two of you knowing how you want to be perceived and treated by each other's families, both individually and as a new couple. You must be strong for each other. Also, emphasis needs to be placed on being honest with each other about how you feel about your own and each other's families of origin.

A little introspection here is what's needed. Each one of you needs to go back and **first** examine how you feel about your **own** family of origin and then move on to your partner's. For example:

- [ ] How deep are my feelings of like, love, or dislike for them?
- [ ] How important do you want to make each family of origin in your new married life?
- [ ] Does that level of importance work well with your partner?
- [ ] How often do you want to see them?
- [ ] Will it be an intrusion when they come to be with you or when you are expected to be with them?
- [ ] Do you want to spend money from your new family budget on them in terms of gifts, occasions, care etc. and how extravagant will those amounts be?
- [ ] If there have been problems, do you want to cut off relations all together? Will that benefit you both in the long-run?

Once each one of you is comfortable with the parameters you've set regarding your own feelings towards your own families of origin, then you must sit and discuss them. Does your partner feel comfortable with what you want regarding your family of origin? Do you feel comfortable with what your partner wants regarding the manner in which he/ she would like you to accept and be with his /her family of origin? If your views are on the opposite sides of the spectrum, can you compromise? Is there a middle ground? Maybe you need to go back and re-examine once again. Family issues can really become nightmares. When they are unforeseen, they can destroy. A simple thing like knowing ahead of time that your partner won't freak out if you decide not to attend a family function on his side can help save a lot of heartache. Take time with this. Stop and think.

Discussion points:

- Are we willing and wanting to see and call ourselves a new family and act accordingly?
- How important is my family of origin to me?
- Is my family of origin more important to me than my new partner in terms of life decisions?
- How much influence are we willing to let either family of origin have on our new family?
- How does my partner feel about my family of origin? How do I feel about his?
- Is it my requirement that my partner make my family of origin equally as important to him as they are to me?

- How much time per week, per month are we willing to spend with either partner's family of origin?
- If they live far away, how much money and time will we allot for travel to see them? How about for them to visit us?
- How much of our budget will be used for familial gifts?
- How will it impact my marriage and me if I'm not well liked by my partner's family?
- Do you view your partner as having enough maturity to put you first before any familial request?

Along with the FAMILY topic comes some FAMILY subtopics, which you should also address.

HOLIDAYS

Holidays are a fact of life. For some people they are joyous occasions, for others they are simply to be tolerated. First off, try to get in touch with how you actually feel about holidays. Remember, really think about it. No blind sentiments. Really introspect. <u>Only from having a true and honest knowledge of your own feelings towards anything, can you sincerely take a stand on it either way</u>. Once you fully know your stance on holidays, then start to think of holidays in terms of how the two of you will spend them. Will the holidays be spent with your family of origin? Will they be spent with his? If it is yes to either question, is it because you *want* to or because you *have* to? Do you think you'd like to simply wish both sides a happy holiday and start your own traditions like staying in your own home or going away? If you stay at home, do you want family of origin to come over? If so, whose? These issues are very important. They can either create a loving holiday atmosphere or completely ruin it for all involved. You can either embark on a steady downfall of unwanted yearly holiday commitments or not. Remember, if you start a *tradition*, let's say of going to either or both sides for a holiday, it becomes harder and harder to "break" these traditions without a lot of flack from someone.

Will either or both of your families of origin accept your new decisions? Are they open and willing to make changes, or are they staunchy and demanding of your presence at holiday time?

The holiday issue compounds if and when you have children. It becomes increasingly difficult to cart, not only yourselves and your children, but all the equipment involved...food, diapers, highchair, changes of clothes, stroller, etc. Think this through before you really begin to make the ritual year after year. Again, before you start to resent it.

Discussion Points:

☐ How do we want to spend our holidays?

☐ Do we even want to celebrate at all?

☐ If we start a tradition of being with family of origin now, are they willing to let us change that if our needs and wants change in the future? Are we strong enough as our own family to make that change happen?

☐ Will we resent not having started our own tradition?

☐ Are our decisions on how we want to handle holidays being respected?

GIFT BUYING

Picture this…

"Hon, it's my mom's birthday, didn't you buy a gift?"
"Did you send a card?" Uh oh, need I say more? What
may seem like such a small expectation on his part can
become one gigantic argument. Husband meant no harm,
but he did expect something to be done. Without ever
having discussed it, he expected that his wife was going to
be responsible for this aspect of the marriage! If a partner
hears the above quoted remark and is in just the right
mood, at just the right time, guess what's going to happen!
Identify those seemingly benign expectations and address
them now so there are relatively no surprises, so there will
be relatively no resentments.

Discussion points:

- ☐ Will you each buy gifts for your own relatives?
- ☐ Is one of you the designated buyer and card sender?
- ☐ Will these gifts be elaborate, stingy, midstream?
- ☐ Do you want to eliminate gifts for relatives and politely ask them to eliminate gifts for you?
- ☐ Identify traditions that exist in both of your histories and work with them. Modify, add, and subtract accordingly.

RELOCATION

You might be thinking why is she placing relocation under this topic and not under the "jobs" topic?

I place this under the "family" topic because extended family and how they feel and how they can influence you regarding relocation can make coming to a decision much more difficult. If you're like some, you've branched out on your own already. Perhaps you've accepted a job that already included a relocation. Or if you're like others, you come from a very close or ethnic family and have either consciously or subconsciously decided to stick around. Either way, first you need to decide whether taking a job far away from family, whether out of want or need, is in the picture for you, for your partner? This can be quite traumatic to some, especially a female who is very close to her family of origin. She may actually persuade her husband not to accept a possibly great position because of her ties to her family of origin. It can be equally traumatic to partners who need to turn down positions based on their partners' need. This is a significant source of resentment. This topic needs to be discussed...

Discussion points:

- ☐ Do either one of you want, contemplate, or completely discount relocation away from place of birth, "home" or away from family of origin?
- ☐ Do you think that either of your families of origin might try to hinder such a move? Will they or can they make things really difficult?

- Is either of you already looking forward to such a move? Is this something either one of you are already counting on doing?

You two really need to be in sync here because relocation is a very real option in today's world. Find out now how each other stands on this subject. No surprises!

These were just some major topics that might arise regarding "Family". There might be others that have occurred with you or that will occur. Don't let them slide. Address them in this fashion.

Let's move on now to the next topic.

SOCIALIZING

FRIENDS

Begin by defining the word *friend*. What does *friend* mean to you? When you discuss friends, specify whether or not they are your friends or your partner's friends. Are they friends that we make as individuals or as couples?

Let's start from the beginning. By now you both have categorized friends by mine, yours, ours, etc. Now define for each other what *friend* means to you. Does *friend* mean good times and fun for you? Does it mean deep connections, do or die for? Is it the same for both of you? Will your partner understand about the way you feel about his/her friends? Does your partner really want your friend to become his friend or is he just doing it for you? Many times a partner will befriend your friend simply out of courtesy, all the while really not liking that person. Then, when an argument arises, out of anger, your partner might say something hurtful about that person. Eliminate this by being honest. Don't just assume he is going to like your friend or that she will like yours. Is it ok to keep a friend that your partner hates? How will you accommodate to his hatred of this friend? What criteria will constitute whether or not a friend or friends will become friends that you'll now fraternize with as a couple?

In the socialization arena, you also need to discuss whether or not the two of you want to have a social life that involves a few friends or a lot of friends. What does social life mean to you? Does it mean a few nights out with friends or a lot of nights out with friends? He might be Mr. Party and you are a pajamas, rent a movie, and eat a pizza on a Saturday night kind of gal. This will pose a big problem. In our relationship, my husband was insistent on many friends, many gatherings, and many social events. I blindly went along with this, had fun on occasion, but as the years went by, I harbored more and more frustration because I felt I was acting or reacting falsely. I was sick of entertaining. I was sick of spending money with, for, or on other people. I was sick of not receiving what I thought to be proper reciprocation, and I was sick of him asking me why I couldn't just enjoy it all more. He enjoyed it, I didn't. Classic difference of opinion. But because I hadn't communicated those feelings, resentments harbored.

Discussion points:

- ☐ Do you mind if each other keeps your single friends? Discuss a time allotment to offer these friends *so that your partner doesn't feel left out*. Do these friends have to become both of your friends?
- ☐ Agree to not feel badly if one or the other doesn't want to share friends for whatever reason.
- ☐ Talk about whether one or the other expects a partner to be a real entertainment mogul? If so, is this acceptable? If it is, who pays for the extras involved with entertaining? Who does the work? Who cleans up? What type of entertaining?
- ☐ Know ahead if one or the other is a home-on-the-weekend kind of person and/or is the other a let's-go-out kind of person. After you're married, your desires for social events might change either to

more or less. Try to discuss how you'll accommodate to each other should this happen.

- ☐ Will your partner mind if you give up precious together time to be with friends?
- ☐ Will your partner allow for how you define friend? Will he/she think you're odd for either giving your all to friends or for giving hardly anything?
- ☐ Have there been any problems with friend issues that have come up already? Don't let them harbor. Bring them up and address them now.

SOCIAL SITUATIONS

How does your partner "act" in social situations? Do you like how your partner acts in a social setting? Does it make you proud? Do you puff up and say to yourself, yep, he's mine. Or do you cringe at what he/she will do or say next?

You have no idea how many "fights" will occur in the aftermath of social situations. Ask yourself honestly:

- ☐ Does he/she act like a know-it-all?
- ☐ Is he loud or obnoxious?
- ☐ Does he offer nothing to the conversation and you feel like you have to be the only talker?
- ☐ Does she flirt?

Pay close attention to what you like or what you don't like about each other in social settings. We know in our minds what we would like to see, or at least what we don't want to see. Bring it to light and compromise on it. Disagreeable social behavior will not magically go away after you're married. It will, however, get more and more annoying. You want to be proud, not embarrassed.

This all sounds harder than it really is. The key is to just bring these topics to light **now**, before they creep up on you and possibly cause a big problem. Before we move on, I would like to interject this point for you to once again ponder and understand. Within all of these topics, the one recurring theme that is the root <u>cause</u> for many of our triggers is the **unmet expectation**. I'm defining "triggers" as something that sparks a heated discussion/argument. As we pointed out before, not discussing something, not bringing an expectation, feeling, want or situation to light, causes expectations to stay within, to remain unspoken, but still very much alive. If these expectations are not brought forth in a constructive manner BEFORE the event takes place, they go unfulfilled and the resentments then build and build. As the resentments build, so does the marital tension. You see, if we had no expectations from our partner, or the relationship at all, then, of course, there would be no resentments. There would be nothing to cause us disappointment, so there would be nothing to get upset at. Of course, having no expectations at all is not possible. We need certain standards by which to measure all things and to live by. Most of the time our expectations of our partner have nothing to do with moral issues of measurement, they are simply **our** measurement of what **we** want or the way **we** think things should be. And that's where the problems begin. We need to have the expectations, the pictures in our minds of how we would like things to be. Our mental pictures show us what we think is correct and good for us and our relationship. This gives us a workable ground, a foundation with which to begin a compromise. The foundation to then say, this is how **I** see it. Partner says, this is how **I** see it and we begin from there. The trick is to SAY IT. Voice those mental pictures before they become shattered, before they are unfulfilled, before they become resentments. Let's say that the expectation does go unfulfilled, it's not too late. Just don't let it fester. Talk about it. Get it out in the open, understand why, and move on.

All these topics that we're discussing are life stuff. We all have a set of expectations for this life stuff. We have formed our expectations about them through our upbringing, society, education, and personal beliefs. We all have them. No matter how we acquired them, we need to express them. The problem occurs when the matter at hand that is causing some marital upset hits us in the face without having been discussed or even alluded to before. By doing what you're doing here, you can possibly avoid that problem.

Bring it to light NOW, before you're faced with a dilemma. Also, don't restrict yourselves to just the topics that are presented here. Once you understand the gist of what we're trying to help you do, you'll recognize different situations or subjects that are significant to your life and a light should go off. You should stop and do exactly what you're doing now with whatever subject matter comes up that you think pertinent to your relationship. Stop and introspect……..if I don't express this expectation, will it eventually cause a disappointment, will it cause a resentment? If you think it will, then say it. Bring it out in the open.

Let's move on…

CHILDREN

CHILDREN

Here, you must first really soul search yourself. Honestly decide whether or not **you** would like to have children. Maybe this is something you know about yourself already, maybe not. But first be sure of your own viewpoint. Don't just take for granted that because your parents had children and your parents' parents had children that you're going to have children. Once again, don't enter blindly. Introspect.

Deciding together on whether or not to bring children into the world is secondary. I remember as a single person always saying to myself that I didn't want children. I didn't want the pain, and I didn't want the bother. I had been brought up in an abusive setting, so I just didn't want anything to do with the whole scene. But as the years went by, my husband and I fell into very traditional roles and before you know it, having children was just the next logical thing. Do I love my children? More than life itself. Have I found the whole experience rewarding? Absolutely. Had we stopped and talked and really brought all matters to light regarding having children, instead of just kind of falling into it, would our choice have been different? It is possible.

The point being is that we did **not** sit and really talk this out. We did not attack the subject matter from every conceivable, logical aspect. I did not introspect. You might be thinking, well if you had approached it that way, you might not have had children and denied yourself the whole experience based on too logical an approach. That could have been the case, but again, a logical approach and an open discussion did not take place and that's where the resentment could stem from. This is an extremely sensitive subject.

Don't approach it with infatuation alone. Some of you think that because the two of you have this magical aura of love, and that when you gaze in each other's eyes you see the universe unfolding in the shape of a newborn. Think again. Having children is not the only next logical step. Stop and think and talk. Consider the ramifications of taking this step. Am I saying don't have children? Absolutely not. What I am saying is consider the whole picture first. Maybe the whole picture hasn't been laid out for you. Come to think of it, it would be impossible to lay it out in its entirety. At the very **least**, use these discussion points to familiarize yourselves a little bit more with the subject of children vs. no children.

Discussion points:

- □ Do I, as my own person, want children?
- □ Do we, as a partnership, want to bring children into this world?
- □ Are we willing to spend our time, energy, money, brainpower, emotions, and the rest of our lives, devoted to another human being rather than to ourselves?
- □ Do we, together, want to feel the ultimate love that a human can feel, which along with its exhilaration, brings vulnerability and susceptibility, and might I add a touch of poverty?

- Who will ultimately have care for your child? I don't mean changing a diaper or two; I'm talking day-in and day-out care. Feeding, washing, playing, teaching, putting to sleep, seeing to schoolwork, driving around, dealing with friends, discipline.
- Will either one of you forfeit your careers? For how long? To see a partner flourish in a career while you are "stuck" at home, over the years, can really cause resentment.
- Do you agree on outside caregiving?
- Do you agree on how to discipline children or will you really surprise one another on this one?
- If you decide you want children, how many?
- How much influence are you willing to let your family of origin have with your children?
- Which one of you will have ultimate decision for naming the child?

Let me give you an example of this. I had three children. I chose three names that I loved. My husband hated all three. My hidden expectation was for him to let me name the children because, let's face it, I did most of the gestational work. But, he didn't make any gestures in that direction. So, without bringing my expectation to light, I harbored an unmet expectation and, although years have gone by, I still hold a strong resentment that I did not name my children what I wanted to name them. You're saying, yes, but if you had named them the names you wanted, then husband would have had the resentment. True. But the major point here is that I didn't even express how strongly I felt about those names and the fact that I really thought he should have let me choose considering the fact that I brought those babies into the world.

I had the expectation, I did not bring it to light, it went unfulfilled, therefore I will always resent it. Don't let this happen to you.

- □ Should the two of you die, you need to have agreed upon whom you will designate as guardians. Don't be surprised when it's time to fill out a last will and testament that you are each thinking of different people. Knowing each other's feeling on this especially delicate issue is crucial.
- □ After your childbearing is over, who will be the one to take care of ultimate birth control? Is he willing to undergo a vasectomy? Will you have to be the one to take care of having a tubule ligation? Pills? Does this fit into either of your religious beliefs?

I need to include this last subject along with this topic. This is extremely delicate, but, there are times when having known each other's feelings beforehand in regards to this is advantageous. I'm speaking about abortions. This procedure is not just limited to instances that occur out of wedlock. Some people I know, during the course of their marriage, for reasons like financial instability, lack of desire to be a parent, or lifestyle issues taking place like going to school or changing jobs, have decided to abort. Believe it or not, an abortion during wedlock is an even greater difficulty because you deal with a different kind of guilt. The guilt that comes from knowing you really have the setting necessary, (a marriage) for this child, but know you don't want it.

Out of wedlock or during your marriage, the thought of wanting or needing an abortion is not an easy thing, but you really should discuss it so you know where the two of you stand on the matter.

VACATIONS

VACATIONS

At last! A fun topic to touch upon. Nothing heavy here, right? Right. Except when HE wants to rent a cottage at the beach for two weeks with his family of origin consisting of 25+ people and your jaw drops!! Hey, it can happen. And maybe it's OK with you if it does happen. The saving grace, however, again, is to know upfront.

Even a seemingly simple subject like vacations comes equipped with its share of ability to cause marital havoc. Vacations can be fun and exhilarating, but, if you're not on the same wavelength or at least close by, even this can throw you. Read and review.

Are you the type of person who may, at some point, like a vacation alone? Will your partner have a problem with this? Do you have a particular group of friends that you have been vacationing with and want to continue vacationing with? Perhaps you and your family of origin have always taken a certain vacation together, will you continue? Is partner willing to have this be part of your lifestyle? Do you each have a preference to a warm or cold climate? Are you going to want to take children with you on all vacations? Does your partner ski, swim, scuba dive, golf? Will he/she want theme vacations to cater to these sporting hobbies? What's your vacation budget?

Discussion points:

- ☐ The above paragraph lists enough questions/scenarios for you to deliberate on. Please touch upon them as well as digesting this. Do not just blindly agree, make your feelings known!

Each item above should be discussed and weighed against its importance and how much it will make one partner happy versus making the other miserable. What may start out as compliance to "make your significant other happy" may in the end, make you feel terrible. (Kind of what I did with the children's names). This will cause strife within yourself and you'll build up resentment. Be honest. But let's face it, there is room for flexibility on all marital decisions, especially this one.

CLOTHING

CLOTHING

Sound stupid? Ha, think again. This can be cause for many a battle. Do you each dress the way the other likes? Don't cover up just to not hurt feelings. You must be honest on both ends. Maybe he/she doesn't like certain styles that you do like. Does she dress too sleazy at times? Maybe he dresses too outdated at times? Talk it out. This is truly one of those aspects of marriage that we just don't think is important enough to get into a discussion about, or we don't want to hurt our partner's feelings so we remain mute on clothes issues that really bother us.

After 28 years of marriage, I still say to my husband at times "Could you please not wear those?" "You look really terrible in them." He might say, "You know, you're right." Or he might say "I like them." In which case we need to reaffirm our feelings. Is your significant other (I'm referring specifically to the guys here) able to pick out his clothes or will he rely on you to buy and put them together for him? That might be cute for a while, but will you resent it? The last thing a wife wants is to view her husband as a "child" who needs his clothes purchased and laid out for him. How about a budget for clothing? Girls, will Honey flip out when you spend X amount on an item of clothing, makeup, shoes, etc.? Right from the beginning, you need to be honest and open with each other.

For example: I expect you (my partner) to look like this when you are around my parents and like this when we're at a business function. You might be thinking that this is ridiculous. You're thinking that you both should have the right to look as you choose. In theory that is absolutely correct, but in actuality, no matter what, our mind's eye sees each other a certain way. We expect it so we need to voice it in order to eliminate any resentments that may occur after the fact. I'm not saying that you have to mandate each other's wardrobe. I think you know what I'm saying. Simply a voicing of an expectation.

Discussion points:

- Do you like each other's style?
- Do you wish something could be different? Speak up now!!!
- Decide on the fact that each other can spend X amount on clothing without having to report to the other. If the item is over a certain amount (you pick the amount) should we discuss it first?
- Will you each keep credit cards for retail stores that you like to purchase at?
- Decide on a dollar cap for those cards and who or how the bill gets paid.
- If your mom buys me clothing that I hate, will you be mad if I return it?
- Really listen to each other without getting angry regarding how each other would like to see the other dressed. This goes for any setting. From bathing suit preference to nightwear. Listen to each other.

Another great benefit of voicing our expectations is that we give our partners a chance to fulfill them! "Clothing" is truly a scenario where you can grant each other's little requests in order to fulfill some of those expectations. If partner would like you to wear a certain type of, let's say, undergarment, why not indulge? Making each other happy by sometimes causing each other's mental pictures to spring to life is unbelievably important in a marriage.

HOBBIES

HOBBIES

Under this topic, the word hobbies encompasses more than just golf on Sunday. This topic, as you will see, holds within it the you that **exists**, the you that existed pre-couple. Who you are and what life is in your little corner, that's what I'm speaking of here. Golf on Sunday goes a lot deeper than just what it seems. It is of astronomic proportions in its importance to married life because it is WHO YOU ARE.

The single worst thing that two people in a relationship can do is this: Lose their own personas to accommodate to being a couple. What do I mean? Just this. You are an individual, you meet up with another individual and the two of you mesh, fall in love, decide to spend your lives together, and boom, you forget who you once were, what you once did, how you once spent free time. Subconsciously you become only a half of a whole. You must never lose your individuality. This is what was attractive to your partner to begin with. Yes, you do combine to create a new entity, but first and foremost you are YOU! You have likes, dislikes, dreams, thoughts, theories, HOBBIES, and desires. You may paint, you may read, golf, play tennis, bird watch, write poems, do carpentry, garden, collect stuff, study world religions, love to work at your job, or any number of other things.

But the point is, these are the things that make up who you are. They are what you do and they represent your life. Why give up these enjoyments you have found in your life? Am I saying be staunch and hard and never change your hobby schedule for your partner? Am I saying to keep going out every weekend because that's what you did before becoming a couple? Come on, of course not. What I am saying is that you need to BE; to just be and be yourself. If you lose that under some pretense of what's good for the relationship, then sooner or later it will come back to haunt you in the form of, yes, once again, resentment. Remember one resentment builds upon another and then, poof, anger and possibly hatred set in.

Now girls, don't take what I'm about to say the wrong way but… I base my assumption here in our nurturing way and our supposed predestination in life to be the givers. But we, typically and I repeat, typically, are the ones who, because we find ourselves in a relationship which might include wife, housewife, homemaker, mother, and a vast assortment of other roles, are more prone to giving up our former more individual selves. When we, down the line, realize what we've done, how much we've selflessly given up, when our partners have given up hardly anything, we resent and blame. The only ones we have to blame are ourselves! No one demands that we give up. Giving up our interests, hobbies, jobs, and likes is NOT a prerequisite for a good marriage. Just the contrary! It is our individualism, or self-reliance that will make us more whole and keep him more attracted to us. If giving up unjustifiable portions of what makes you tick IS a prerequisite by your partner then you really need to look at him again and determine why. By the same token, we girls have no right to mandate him giving up what he doesn't want to give up. This means a little compromising and adjusting and understanding must take place. Remember, ladies don't mother him and gentlemen, don't smother her. Don't mother; don't smother.

Discussion points:

- Getting to know your partner's hobbies and interests is fun and exciting.
- Celebrate what makes each other the rounded individual that you love.
- Discuss how much time you each think is a fair amount to devote to your own hobbies.
- Set aside reasonable amounts of time and money to do the things you love. Together or separate. This will strengthen the marriage unbelievably so.
- Try some fun stuff together. It may be cook, golf, hike, ski whatever you like. But from experience, doing some type of recreation together, not just in the early years, but throughout the marriage, really continues to add warmth, spark, and plain old fun.
- If one of you is a "workaholic" and this is, in fact, what makes you happy, does partner realize this? Will partner resent this in the long-run? Are you pretending to make time for fun stuff now and will return to your old workaholic ways after the marriage? It's only fair to be upfront now, before resentments build.

SEXUALITY
AND
SENSUALITY

SEXUALITY

Seems like such a simple straightforward topic within the marital realm, doesn't it? We're married, we have sex, end of discussion. If that is the way you feel, it could also be the end of the marriage.

So very many sub-issues come into play in regards to sex, sexuality, and your sex lives once big, boring marriage comes into the picture and really messes things up or possibly, hopefully makes things much, much better. Let's start at the beginning, shall we. Any sexual relation can be scary these days. You need to empower yourselves with the knowledge of your partner's previous relationships and medical history. If you don't, you're playing with fire, no matter what. An AIDS and STD test should be the norm. None of this "don't you trust me?" Just get it done. With this out of the way, you need to look at **yourself** from a sexual point of view. Not your partner, you. How do you view yourself sexually? Are you sexually attracted to your partner? Some people may love their partners dearly but not really be sexually attracted to them. That may work for some. The importance is in knowing. Some questions to ask yourself also are: How is your current sex life? Do you know your sexual self in terms of likes and dislikes? Do you want and expect certain things?

How open are you in terms of your own sexuality? Are you daring? Armed with a pretty accurate picture of who **you** are sexually, you must approach your partner and discuss yours and his/hers findings. Do they mesh? Are there topics that you need to compromise on? A healthy sex life in a marriage can create and maintain an intimacy that you can achieve in no other way. Now this doesn't mean strictly intercourse; it could mean anything you want it to mean.

I had a very good friend who confided in me that she never had sex on her honeymoon! As odd as that may sound, what was odder is that she didn't give it a second thought! She had never been particularly comfortable with her own sexuality and was really not sexually attracted to her partner. She assumed, never having addressed the matter, that this was normal for her and her partner, and continued on. Unfortunately, it did become the norm for them. It was the beginning of a very rocky sexual aspect to their married life thus giving way to long stretches of non-intimacy, long periods of sexual dysfunction in the form of impotency and non-interest, a lot of frustration, and ultimately a realization that this potentially great part of her marriage stunk. Over the years, communication between her and her husband opened up from a desire to make things work.

Through a lot of communication about what each other wanted, needed, and felt, eventually their sex life gained a sparkle which had never been there in the beginning. If both had been more open to their own sexual feelings right from the start and had relayed those feelings to each other right from day one, as is the intention here, many tears and grief could have been avoided. It's only because of their strong commitment to each other that the marriage survived long enough to enjoy the new found sexual interest. You can argue that new feelings and wants grow over time and there's no way this couple could have talked about everything regarding their sexuality before the marriage. Yes, that's true and is true for all aspects of life and individuals. However, what wasn't done, and ultimately had to take place, which is what I'm stressing here, is that there has to be, number one, introspection. Identify **your** wants. And, number two, state those wants. What do I want to give and get back? Seem selfish? Not when it comes to sexuality. You know why? Because if you're not honest and up front about sexuality, other things too, but especially sexuality, big resentments build up. Resentments that are born out of, in this case, sexual expectations that go unfulfilled. Being unfulfilled then leads to emptiness and a festering desire.

The desire could then become outward, meaning that you will tend to look outside the marriage for the needed satisfaction. This emptiness then causes people's eyes to stray and ultimately causes a severe breakdown in a potentially very intimate and very special part of the marriage. I'm not stating that because you'll discuss sexual topics before the marriage that your marriage is safe from either partner straying, but when it comes to something as intimate and special as what you two share sexually, shouldn't you at least try to curb some possible misunderstandings or lack of fulfillments before they even occur? Maybe a partner wants certain things to take place in his/her sexual life that they're too embarrassed to ask for. If a dialogue opens up regarding sexual wants, that embarrassment might be eliminated. Even if you do discuss sexual wants and desires early on, you really need to keep this subject constantly open throughout the marriage. People change. Preferences change. Everybody wants a change. Keep the lines of communication open. Keep an open mind to the new and different.

What if, however, a partner does have an affair? What will you do? How will you handle finding that love note addressed to your husband or wife?

What will it feel like to hear a story from a friend that your partner was seen being intimate with another? Tell each other what you'll do in that case. Will you automatically end the marriage? Will you want to seek counseling? I know you're thinking, "how will I know how I'll react?" But you know what? I think you do know, and both partners should let each other know.

Don't just think because you are sexually active or feel yourself pretty normal in this area that all will be well in the marriage bed, you must, must talk about what you expect sexually before you find yourself in a situation that can ruin what you two share.

Discussion points:

(Don't be shy about these, be as open as possible for your own good and the good of the future of the marriage).

- ☐ Sexually speaking, what do I want? What do I like? What do I like him/her to do? Do I feel that I can ask this of him/her?
- ☐ What kind of sexual drive do I have? Does partner have? Are they in sync?
- ☐ How frequently do I or my partner like to have sex?

- How will we handle a period of impotency or non-interest should it come along?
- Is my partner willing to try new things; the approaches which may be a little daring? Am I?
- What can start off very strong can dwindle with time, fatigue, children, etc. How will we handle that? By the same token, what may not be very important right now in the relationship can become very important at some point. Are we prepared for these possible changes?
- What are his or her limits?
- Make each other feel comfortable enough to tell partner the kinds of things you'd like to try out.
- Are your desires and wants shared or does he/she want nothing to do with them?
- How will you handle it if I stray?
- Let each other know that you are willing to listen to anything and that you won't embarrass or humiliate your partner.

SENSUALITY

Human sensuality is very important. We, as a society, tend to be very rushed, hurried, always on the go, leaving very little time for small showings of affection. However, these small affirmations of how much I love my partner and how much my partner loves me, are so very important. These affirmations include a variety of notions. They can range from a simple look, a wink, hugs and kisses, a warm touch, a pat, or even the simple act of looking into each other's eyes. These acts can soothe and affirm and bring down another's defenses and make trivial and not so trivial problems seem more tolerable. Some of us need more and want more open signs of affection, verbal, physical or otherwise. Some of us don't.

When we want or need these signs of affection and don't receive them in return, or we give them and they're not accepted the way we think they should be, we once again build resentments. We battle out in our minds the negativity associated with our partners not acting how we think being sensuous and affectionate should be. We feel slighted, possibly unloved, and a small marital breakdown occurs.

You both really need to be in touch with this aspect of your personas for your own well-being and for the good of the relationship.

This is something that I bet is hardly ever brought to light until a problem results. Take a moment to examine what you'll want and what partner would like. Remember, when a relationship is fresh and new, in most cases, we tend to touch, kiss, and hold each other a lot so we don't often think about how things will be down the line a bit. Human nature is such that those gestures tend to dwindle with time, but do they have to be eliminated? Find out how each other feels about sensuality and affection. Keeping sensuality alive in the marriage might get a little tough over the years when so many other things take precedence. Discuss it. Make a pact to keep it alive. Do whatever works for the two of you, but in order to do that, you will have to have talked about it first.

Discussion points:

- How often do I like to be told that I'm loved? How often do I like to say it?
- How affectionate am I? Do I like, on a day-to-day basis, a lot of affection and the showing of affection?
- Do I like a lot of hugs and kisses and reminders of my partner's love for me? Do I not?
- Is my partner an affectionate person or more standoffish?
- Will I or my partner misinterpret a lack of outward affection as a lack of love? Preempt that now if that's not the case.

Tell each other what you want or need because at the end of the day in your new life as husband and wife, if partner greets you with a cursory "Hello" and goes about his/her business and you're left with empty, open arms and no kiss, you will begin to question his/her love or lack thereof. That outward sign of lack of affection could be misinterpreted as a lack of love. If you realize that you're both equally affectionate, go for it. If your needs are different in this end of your own sensuality, will this cause trouble? Just knowing will be enough to allay any fears or resentments. You'll walk into this knowing, OK I like kissing and hugging and holding and touching and caressing and having my hair massaged but he/she doesn't. How can we compromise? Are we worth it to each other to give in and or hold back so as not to hurt or be hurt? The key is, once again, that you are aware. Nothing gets harbored; nothing gets added to your list of "things I hate that he/she does or doesn't do."

RELIGION

RELIGION

Treading on sacred ground can be real tough. Going into your marriage, you bring with you years of religious history, familial influence, personal preference, and a whole host of other outside influences to contend with. Once again, you as an individual must come to a realization about what part religion plays in your own life, first. You need to ponder and answer these types of questions, which you may or may not have already done. Do I want or have a religion? Do I want that religion to be part of my married life? How does practicing MY religion in OUR marriage rate on the importance scale. Religious views can change throughout your life, but for right now, you need to have a starting point. You need to both bring some religious viewpoints to the marital table. If you're both religion-free and you've made that known then continue on, but always remember to keep an open mind to what your partner may become interested in someday. Alike-religion marriages have an advantage, of course, but don't just take for granted that you'll simply continue on this same path because that's what you've always done. Once again, start fresh by asking your new family (the two of you) whether or not this is the route you want to take. Couples from different religious backgrounds really need to introspect.

Keeping separate religions is definitely doable. Many people have done it. Respect and appreciation of each other and of each other's beliefs weigh heavily here. The point, once again, is to not walk into this new phase of life without having stopped and questioned. Do I want to continue on my religious path? What role will we choose for religion to play in our lives? Stop, ask, think, and talk about it. Be open and aware that changes can always take place.

Discussion points:

- Do I WANT a religion?
- What do I want from a religion? What do I want that religion to give to the marriage?
- How important of a role do you want religion to play in the marriage?
- If my partner is not as religious as I, will I require him to become such before I will be happy in a marriage? (Don't ever hope for and bank on the fact that your partner will miraculously see the light and convert to your religion after you're married. If, in fact, that doesn't happen, you'll be thrown into a big resentful situation.)
- If you're from two different religious backgrounds, how will children be raised if you decide to have them?
- How will religious holidays be spent?
- Does it matter to you if your partner's family of origin is of a different religion and resent you and your religion?
- If you have the same religion but different churches, temples, etc., which one will you choose to attend?

Get the religion aspect of your marriage settled right away. If not, resentments will enter the union sooner or later. This is heavy stuff. Do not let it come between the two of you. It is not worth it. All it takes is a little introspect and communication.

MONEY

MONEY

The subject of money, even though we don't want to admit it, is probably bigger than all of the previous subjects. Why? Because without money, there is no survival. With it, there is a constant differing of opinion regarding all aspects that surround it.

There is the possibility of endless arguments about it. Or, if planned correctly, this aspect of married life could be quite solid and productive just like, as I mentioned previously, a business. Respect it, talk about it, plan around it, have meetings about it and it won't cause strife. Leave it unto itself without addressing it and it will fester and cause havoc in you marital lives. You need to be aware of money stuff, both simple and intricate. For example, very basic, of course, who earns what? What are your salaries? Who spends more? On what should it be spent? How much should be saved? How will you save it?

In a communal home, there are communal things. Money becomes one of those things. But it is probably the hardest thing to share. WE earn it, WE work hard for it when it comes to how WE spend it or how WE handle our finances, everything's cool. When it comes to someone else handling our money for different uses, or even worse, telling us how we should handle **our** money, the pretty picture begins to cloud.

If there is one part of a communal married life you need to discuss, it is, without a doubt, money and all of the ramifications surrounding the use of money. A lack of knowledge about money and the role that it plays in your new married life is a recipe for disaster. You must acquaint yourselves as fully as possible with the monetary part of this relationship. Do you know what each other earns? In many cases, the female earns more than the male. Is this going to bother either one of you? Does the amount that each other earns satisfy the other? What I mean by satisfy is, does the partner feel that the other is earning to their full potential? Do you feel YOU are at your earning potential for right now or do you need to put effort into your career? How will that impact your marriage—travel time, late nights? Does your partner respect what you do and what you earn? Does the partner feel that both are bringing the most that they can to the table? If one partner feels he/she is carrying the load and feels this to be a burden then resentments will occur. Is one of you a spender and one a miser? Are you both spenders and should you receive counseling before things get out of hand? Do either one of you own assets like stock, property, CDs, etc. that might require a prenuptial agreement? Has a last will and testament been discussed? Will you have one drawn?

Along with the tedium of daily life comes the tedium of monthly bills. Who will handle the bills? Have you come up with a budget for your new home life or will spending be haphazard? Make the decision now that you'll both sit down and set up a household budget before even the first week of marriage. The budget should show what comes in and what goes out. This alone will eliminate many problems. To not do this, is to invite arguments. Do you differ on your opinions on products being bought new or used? Will you become a one-income family once children arrive? Who will be the income provider if one decides to stay home? Even something as small as clipping coupons can cause riffs! Picture this, husband says, " my mother used to clip coupons for her weekly grocery shopping, how come you don't?" That simple sentence can cause a full-blown argument. But, its roots are sincere. If he views one of her contributions to the family budget as saving money weekly by using coupons and she views it as a waste of time, then resentments can build. There needs to be a constant refinement of details.

You couldn't possibly review all monetary situations before entering a marriage, but you absolutely, positively should start with the above questions and this checklist. You will save yourself and your marriage a ton of strife if you walk into it knowing AT LEAST these items.

As with all the topics we've discussed, including and especially this one, keep an open line of communication at all times and even set specific times aside for discussions relating to specific money topics. For example, how much should we spend on holiday gifts this year? How are we doing with our savings? Is it time to think about an investment? By doing that, you will not only contribute greatly to the strength of the marriage, but also eliminate many, many possible arguments.

Discussion points:

First go back and reread this topic. Many important discussion points were already mentioned. Don't leave any unaddressed. You'll wish you hadn't.

- Will one or both of you "handle" the money?
- Find out what each other earns (if you don't already know).
- Talk about your aspirations as far as your earnings go. Do you want to aspire to earn more? Are you comfortable with where you are and have no desire to "climb?" You might be thinking that partner will grow in his/her career and that for he/she to climb is important to you. Partner might be very comfortable right where he/she is and have no desire to climb. Surprise!
- Will you be naming each other as beneficiaries?
- Will one of you stop working after children?
- What will you use as savings vehicles?
- Do either one of you own assets: land, property, CD's, money markets, stock, 401K's, savings accounts? Are you willing to share those with your new partner?
- Do you need a prenuptial agreement?
- Do you want to make investing something you do together or will one of you handle this?
- Will you set up a checking/savings account jointly? Keep them separate?
- How do you both feel about credit cards? Will you have limits?
- Who will you name as second beneficiaries?
- Please sit down and formulate a monthly budget, this will save so much time and anguish on both your parts.
- Decide now whether one or both of you will do the actual paying of bills every month.

- Is one of you the type who will take out a loan to purchase and the other the type that saves before the purchase?
- How much of each paycheck will be kept as pocket money?

Money, money, money! I can't tell you how important this subject will be in your marriage. Really try to make this subject one that is regularly discussed all throughout your marriage. The key is to not discuss money just when there is a problem, but to maintain discussions about it on an ongoing basis. Be sure to especially treat this aspect of your marriage like a business. Constant alignment of monetary issues will keep things running much smoother.

Do you still want to get married? Just kidding, of course you do. Probably even more now that you know so much more about yourself and your partner. Have you gone through and just read this book or have you actually discussed it? The option is obviously yours. I congratulate you if you've taken the time to introspect and discuss. You and your marriage will only benefit from this. You'll see as marital life unfolds that countless topics will arise that need to be discussed. These are just some major ones. The key is honesty, respect each other's opinions, and keep the open lines of communication. Sound easy? Hopefully, it will be easier after this book. Above all, never attack or blame, or at least try not to! It's impossible to foresee every scenario that could possibly play out and how you would handle each one.

But, to walk into these delicate issues, which I can almost guarantee will eventually take place, without having discussed them, is like walking through a mine field and hoping that you'll both be OK when you reach the other side. Preparation is the key. Use these discussions as tools to begin an even happier life. Will all these subjects apply to all people? No, of course not. However, many will, because most marital issues are universal.

Add your own subjects to those already discussed, like grocery shopping, cooking, chore sharing, car maintenance, late office hours, business trips, schooling. More and more "items for discussion" will pop up as your early marital years unfold. Don't harbor. Discuss, be adaptive and flexible, and then discuss some more!

Good luck, have fun but most of all soul search. Really be honest with yourself and your partner. And remember . . .

PREVENT THE RESENT!

Prevent resentment from even starting to take shape by stating your expectations very openly. Don't ever think that your partner can automatically know your wants and needs. If you think along those lines, then many of these issues will come back to haunt your relationship.

Hope you've enjoyed reading this humble little book as much as I have enjoyed writing it. Marriage can be a wonderful, intimate gem in our short lives. Treasure it. Congratulations!

FOOD FOR MARRIAGE THOUGHTS THAT CAN'T BE STRESSED ENOUGH

NEW FAMILY

Emblazon in your minds that you are now a new family unto yourselves. Even though you may not have started "the family" by having children, you must realize that the two of you are a new entity now. This may sound simple but it is a difficult concept. By realizing and accepting this, you automatically will command respect for your new family from those who are important to you. Without this realization on your part, you won't place enough importance on the two of you being a new family and you won't reap as many benefits from it. What do I mean? For example, I think especially for women, there is a tendency to still look to your family of origin for support, acceptance, and guidance. That's OK. But what's even better is to really stop, introspect and see that your new partner is really the one to whom you should turn to for those things. Place an importance on the two of you. Make this new entity the hub. In doing so, you will make the marriage stronger and healthier. The bond between you needs to be made stronger every day. Turning to each other for things you might have turned to others for before is a good way to strengthen your relationship. Making demands for yourselves as a unit and looking inwards to your own needs as that unit instead of what others need from you, will strengthen it too.

Does this mean to make yourselves an island and forsake all others? No. It simply means you need to place the importance on the new marriage that it deserves. Step back and take stock of what you now have. Do that often. Never take it or your partner for granted….never.

GIVE and TAKE

How's that for cliché? A very simple concept, but yet, in my opinion, it is the whole foundation that a marriage is built upon. The give and take in a marriage is an underrated and misunderstood concept. Underrated because its importance has been downplayed, and misunderstood because even though you may have been told that marriage is a "two way street," you haven't been taught how it works. Marriage is a constant give and take. Picture a seesaw, if you will; now picture the two of you on the seesaw. The seesaw is the marriage and you two are the players. At any given time, one of you might be up and the other down. Then the seesaw tips and the other is up, and you down. Oh, sure there might be times when you've both got your feet firmly planted on the ground and you're sort of coasting along. You feel like you're on the same wave, you're together, you're one. This is a good thing. But, much of the time, one or the other of you will be in need.

It could be that you need emotional support; it could be financial need. It may be a physical need or a spiritual need. There may be career issues that you'll need help with. It may be a family of origin issue or something as simple as a bad day. The need may be in the form of advice, to be listened to whole-heartedly, or to be cared for during a period of sickness. You might need to shut down and go to sleep without worrying about chores, kids, dinner, etc. One of you might feel the need to talk and get something that's been bothering you out in the open. Whatever the reason, when one of you is "needy" and the other is in the position to give (having no needs at that particular time), selfishness must exit the picture. There must, at these times, be no "me" in the picture. This is when the "give" part of give and take comes in. Give of your time and love. There's no greater act of kindness that you can do for your partner. But, make sure this is reciprocated. Always respect and appreciate each other for doing this.

NEVER STOP PLAYING.

Always, always find time to play, to laugh, and to just have fun. This doesn't have to be expensive fun. Wrestle on the floor, go to a playground, swim, take a walk, hold hands, ride your bikes, cook together. Anything!

Keep the fun in the marriage alive. You'll both benefit. If you let it, the work and responsibilities will gobble up the marriage. Don't let that happen. Find time to play.

TREAT THE MARRIAGE LIKE A BUSINESS

What I mean here is not to treat the intangible love part of the marriage like a business. I mean treat the factual, tangible parts of the marriage like a business. Businesses thrive if they are run properly. So will your marriage. My intent is not to sound cold and harsh, but running a marriage, especially after children come into the picture, if they do, can get harder and harder. Set up meeting times to review anything that's of concern like school, work, purchases, vacations, the list is endless. Have an agenda for the meeting. Have separate money/budget meetings. Make sure you use a monthly budget form. Know what comes in and what goes out. Put some unspoken house or kid rules into written form. Keep things as precise as possible in the business side of the marriage. All will run smoother.

Enjoy the precious love that you have found in this turbulent sea of humanity. Nothing can ever come close to the intimacy felt in a marriage. As the years go by, the warmth and love will deepen.

Never stop communicating with each other. Never stop being the best you can be to yourselves and to each other. Remember, it all really will pass by so quickly, immerse yourselves in its beauty.

I dedicate this sweet book to the person I most admire and love, my husband. I thank the gods each day for him. From the here to the hereafter, my love for you, Rick, will forever deepen. Thank you for your love, thank you for everything.

Venice Davidian is currently living and loving in South Carolina. She has been married for twenty-eight years and is mother to three beautiful children.

###

www.ingramcontent.com/pod-product-compliance
Lightning Source LLC
Chambersburg PA
CBHW050538280326
41933CB00011B/1632